POEMS FROM THE DARKROOM

For my loves: Being mother to my sons, Josh and Dylan, has been the highlight of my life. Marrying Joe, the reward. My parents and siblings are the foundational song of my heart. My grandchildren, the charmed encore. Special thanks to Warren Lapine.

©2022 Colleen Redman

All rights reserved. Printed in the United States of America. No part of this book may be used or reproduced in any manner without written permission except for brief quotations for review purposes only.

Poems from the Darkroom

By Colleen Redman

Table of Contents

1. Poems from the Dark Room 7
2. Voice 8
3. The Visitation 10
4. The Origin Story 12
6. Not a Birthmark 14
7. What Else Did He Make? 16
8. The Invoice 18
9. The Wasp 20
10. Vertigo 21
11. Fateful Finds 23
13. My Grandmother's Brogue 25
15. Bio-Note 27
16. Setting Sail 28
17. Lights Out 28
18. In Answer to Katherine's Year of Haiku 30
19. Losing Ground 31
20. I Don't Have 32
21. Dreams Have No Platitudes 34
22. When Sleep Plays Hard to Get 35
23. Stormed -January 2021 36
24. This is Not a Horror Movie 37
25. The Magic Trick 38
26. What Would Carl Jung Say? 39
27. Sunflowers 40
29. When You Come Full Circle 42
30. Hit Publish 44

31. Just When I Think I Have No More Poems to Write 45
32. Open Slowly 46
33. Look Away. 47
34. When We Wait More Than We Write 48
35. Decomposition 49
36. The Older Poet 50
37. Let it Be. 51
38. When Time Doesn't Rhyme 52
39. You Are Here. 53
40. The Scenic Route. 54
41. Ashes to Ashes 55
42. How to Die 57
43. Hibernation 2020 58
44. The Last Dance 59
45. The Final Leaving: How to 60
46. Surprise Endings 61

POEMS FROM THE DARK ROOM

It takes time in the dark room to bring lived-experience into focus and to develop the meaning we've made of our lives.

Imprinted stills
Proof of life
Picked up at the corners
and held to the light

A body of work
made of muscle and flesh
A lost art developed
from a landmarked distance

We hid them to protect them
then forgot where they were
We saw their reflections
and cast them in dreams

Now dredged and named
and hung one by one
We signed their originals
while still recognizable

We captured their honesty
before letting them fade
We saw how they shaped us
frame by frame

VOICE

They say you have to find your voice
like they ask 'what do you want to be
when you grow up?'

But you don't know where to look
or know that you have the voice
you were born with

You sit on the phone
with a boy you like
and time stops still
while no one speaks

You wouldn't tell
that you got locked out
of a house while babysitting
that you had to break a window
to get back in

You don't raise your hand at school
You'd rather not talk
than be wrong

You don't lie
but don't tell the truth
You like your voice
when you sing with the radio
songs of someone else's words

You remember when you talked to yourself
in the blackberry patch
and unleashed the power of speech
on a black widow spider

You remember the bat
tucked between the briars
and the scratches on your legs
from reaching for places you couldn't go

And now you're grown
and you don't remember what you said then
You like your voice but like the quiet
You don't sing along unless you mean it

You add your own words
to the sum of parts
Distinct as fingerprints
A poet's north star

You write it down
and read it out loud
Your thoughts are the medium
and voice is your art

The Visitation

My mother had a red kitchen
with apple and strawberry plates
Before her kitchen was red it was pink
but her life was not rosy

My father had two answers
when asked 'how are you?'
A good day answer was
"I got out of bed
I'm ahead of the game"
A bad day answer was
"It's a rocky boat"

When *he* rocked the boat
my mother helped steady it
My father was fun-loving
and my mother got things done

My kitchens are blue
like the delft blue platter
that my grandmother carried
from Ireland to America
when she was 13 years old and alone

Not blue like stormy weather
but like the quilted jumper
I wore in the first grade
that my mother dressed me in
for school picture day

I imagine my mother's kitchen
still existing somewhere in time
after the big bang
and near a bright galaxy
that a giant telescope can see

The sun pours in on my dad
who is sitting in his favorite chair
at the red gingham covered table
He's ahead of the game
he no longer plays

My mother picks lilacs
from her pink kitchen days
while I sing my heart out
to Neil Young's After the Gold Rush

I watch from a distance
closer than I seem
until I blink like a blue star
bound by its orbit
until I pass like a dream
in my mother's deep sleep

The Origin Story

You wouldn't tell
that you thought you were a mother
when you were three-years-old
that you lived in the Germantown projects
and had a baby carriage for your baby doll

And you wrote 100 poems
before you wrote this one
like a veteran who talks
about everything but the war

You were the mother in the backseat
of the car that drove away
and you were the baby forgotten
in a cabin on the Cape
the one that got left with a family friend
and at the Chelsea Naval hospital
with third degree burns

And where was your comfort
when your baby was left
and when you were the baby
too young to know
that the body holds
its wordless wounds
carries them for a lifetime?

The doll was packed up
and mailed to your house
but you wouldn't touch her
and didn't want her

Later, in school you learned about war
it was taught like math or spelling
as if it was perfectly natural

You had to memorize the dates
of wars that shouldn't have happened
and you carried the weight
of generational trauma

And when asked what super power
you would want if you had one
'to be invisible' you answered

You forgot baby dolls
and moved on to Barbies
You didn't talk to strangers
or wait for heroes

You marched for peace
and cherished children
You wrote your way through
an archeological therapy
that led to the unearthing
of the carriage left empty

Not a Birthmark

"A scar is what happens when the word is made flesh" – Leonard Cohen

The scars around my ankles
from being burned when I was a baby
are almost invisible now
Like the wound of being separated
from mother and home
for a four-week hospital stay

We called dragonflies "sewing needles"
when we were kids at Billington Sea
We were scared they would land on us
pierce our skin and stitch it together
with a glistening thread of web

We thought snakes lived in the mouths
of carrousel horses at Paragon Park
We had to think about where to put our little hands
and what other dangers could be lurking

There once was a paisley-shaped scar
under the left side of my ribcage
I imagined it as a hot splash
that my mother missed
when the dishtowel slipped
and the pot of boiling water crashed
when she covered me with butter
to treat third degree burns
but forgot to take off
my shoes and socks

Two sons and two tracks
across the width of my abdomen
is a tender trust hidden
by stretch-marked flesh
They're sliced side-by-by side

but join together in places
They don't reveal the internal
twisted tissue that clings

Sometimes lives are cut short
Pulled from the world as if from a womb
Two brothers, a sister, a father and mother
have vanished without a trace

In Africa they say 'the blessing is next to the wound'
Rumi says the cracks are where the light enters you
In Japan they mend broken vessels with seams of gold
making the gift and pain both visible
marking the routes to stories turned legacies
held by the strength of life-affirming resiliency

WHAT ELSE DID HE MAKE?

I don't remember the way
to the first mall in the South Shore
to the first McDonalds in Weymouth
or the drive-in movie on Route 3A

But I remember the footpath
through the Japanese knotweed
that we called rhubarb and ate with sugar
behind the old Coast Guard Station
on the way to a friend's house

And the stone concrete jetty
we dried off on after swimming
that we never thought of as a boat launch

I remember being indignant
by a wart on my knee
and the first time I was stung
by a yellow jacket

I remember riding the brakes
going down hills on a bicycle
and choosing the black cowboy hat
over the white one

And the first catechism question
out of a list of sixty-nine
that we memorized and recited
Who made you?

I still remember the flowers in the tall grass
that we didn't know the names of
and the secret that I kept
about eating purple crown vetch

I remember the grass fire my brother started
and the spankings we got from sneaking cookies
the linoleum floor and the crystal fluted doorknobs
in the bedrooms that were cold in winter

I remember the lies I told in confession
because kids have no real sin
and if they did they wouldn't remember them

What else did God make?
God made all things
I always said
"I stole a cookie"

The Invoice

When bras were white
even after Labor Day
before they were burned
for peace and free love
When falsies were tissue paper
stuffed in A cups
a visible slipped strap
was cause for embarrassment

When cigarettes were glamorous
and your mother's closet
was an exotic taboo
where you tore open a sanitary napkin
to see what was inside

When Lucy and Desi slept in twin beds
And children hid under desks during nuclear drills
You played with matches
and picked your favorite Beatle
while your heroes were assassinated
and your brother was drafted

You slathered on baby oil
for the promise of a tan
before napalm babies in Vietnam burned
and 50,000 vets killed themselves

Now we mourn the lost days
when sticks and stones
didn't break our bones
and fires were for burning fall leaves

Now strangers hang their clothes
in your mother's closet

and children hide under desks
so they won't be shot

The American Dream brought
a rude awakening
Our buy now pay later
bills are due

The Wasp

The wasp leaves an unexpected sting
It strikes for no visible reason
and then flies away

There is no justice
as you go through
the stages of suffering
and the slow arrival of relief

You learn to avoid it
and come to expect it
The swelling disappears
But the memory holds on

You don't think you'll ever
trust a wasp again
and all wasps begin
to look the same

The wasp does what it wants to
It follows its instinctive urges
and to a wasp, all people
look the same

Vertigo

My mind is a blizzard in a snow globe
The drifts pile up
Sometimes they lean to one side
The leaks are inevitable
when they melt

I bump into door frames
and hold on to walls
I avoid unplanned moves
Crash but don't fall

It probably started when I fainted
and hit my head on the gym floor
It knocked out my pigment
and set the stage for darkness
when I was thirteen-years old

The doctor told me
'people pay a lot of money
for a white streak like that'
but I missed my brown eyebrow
and sunscreen caused my face to swell

Sometimes the mix-up
helps me speak like a poet
when words come in dizzying display
They land in unexpected order
like square pegs don't fit in round holes

It might have started when I was four-years old
when my father read The Snow Queen to me
He never finished the story
about a sister in search of her brother
Her red shoes floated down the river
I've been looking for them ever since

Vertigo is not an Alfred Hitchcock thriller
Not as bad as a glass shard lodged in your eye
It's more like trying to stay warm in the cold
while searching for ways to describe snow

Fateful Finds

I found poetry on the radio
and moons that dangled
like carrots on sticks

I found God in a picture frame
at the top of the stairs
and a book of fairytales
in a house that is gone

I found rusted metal
butterfly wings
that I keep with a picture
of my older sister

I found a pill
I couldn't swallow
and a footnote
too small to read

I found a vase unearthed
from a backyard dump
Brown like a potato
that survived the blight

Dug from a swamp
that freezes in winter
Carried from house to house
it holds dried flowers
that never wilt

I still find pennies in the dustpan
but not the dimes
that I wanted to put in loafers
to wear in Mrs. Neville's class
to take off under my desk

because summer
was never long enough

Because summer
was never long enough
and our winter mittens
never matched

Our knee socks slipped down
around our ankles
waiting in the cold
at the school bus stop
where I later dreamt
of German shepherds
that wouldn't let me pass

Today I walked down
a different long driveway
and was stopped by an ice puddle
A Narnia's window
A fairy godmother's oracle
too small to skate on

I stood my ground
on the spiraled path
that rippled out
and froze in place

It restored my faith
in a graceful truth
A hardened view
destined to melt
A slip of fate
made beautiful

My Grandmother's Brogue

My grandmother hid her brogue
the way I insert R's
where they used to not exist
in a Rebel South
where folks say "Y'all"
and I say "You guys"
when I let down my guard

My grandmother couldn't hide
her Irish temper
She taught it to my father
who thought its harshness
would make us stronger
But as he got older he learned
that oppression breeds poverty
and poverty brutality

How well we hide
our wounds
constrict our throats
to muffle grief
in every language

"It was for my own good"
"I turned out all right" we say
In a big hole it all goes

We used to think if we dug far enough
we'd get to China
As if we wouldn't come across
all manner of corpses and treasure
As if we could disregard our own family trauma

My Grandmother came to America
to be a servant

and then have 11 children
for the Catholic Church
"Jesus, Mary and Joseph!"

I used to think a brogue was a brooch
a shiny pin I could proudly wear
that would restore me to my rightful status

"Don't shine too bright
You'll attract the thieves
The neighbors will think you're uppity
and surely it's a sin"
was the family inheritance I received

So we hide what is most valuable
along with what is shameful
and after a while we don't
know the difference
between our corpses and our treasures
our brogues and brooches

In a big hole it all goes
But it never goes away

My Grandmother's brogue
grows green in my throat
because what we bury takes root

Bio-Note

I am a poem
that's read from center
from right to left
or end to start

I'm not overgrown
like the forsythia in my yard
and not clipped close
like a landscaper's victim

I'm not an easy catch
but don't play hard to get
I'm best read
with eyes squinted
with head tilted
and feet on the ground

I'm a one and only
best-kept secret
that doesn't claim
to be your favorite

I'm the girl next door
who speaks in metaphor
who doodles and spirals
with a wild streak of blue

I'm a scrap of paper
signed and delivered
an irreplaceable original
to be unfolded and considered

I'm unrehearsed verse
with value that's felt
that appreciates with age
that speaks for itself

Setting Sail

The pioneers have left
for the uncharted New World
They fell off the horizon
when the world was flat

When I was third of nine
in an unbroken family line
before survival was optional
and paradise was a gamble
we had already won

Navigating destiny
with safety in numbers
with a lifetime of chances
and luck that runs out

Now I'm first of six
unanchored from my sidekicks
The children are orphans
marooned from the mainland
and I am an Island
waiting for a ship

Lights Out

I mistook the fireflies for your headlights
coming down the gravel driveway
A distant car on the Parkway
could be yours

I remember waiting for my dad
to come home from work in the rain
and worrying that he wouldn't
during Hurricane Carol in 1953

Now the light fades out
like the end of a life
and I'm sad even in summer
in bare feet with fireflies
that twinkle like stars
trying to jump their way
back to heaven

In Answer to Katherine's Year of Haiku

I
The moon likes to shine
from different angles
It changes its pose
and each one is whole

Not one thing
I say one and move on
like the moon across the sky
I orbit round and back again
Always changed
but the same

II
Don't tell me the moon
is always full
I can see with my own eyes
But half-truths are tricks
and truth can't be fixed
I'm glad I can admit
when I'm fooled

III
Life etches itself
like tattoos I can't hide

Truth is hard enough
and lies are insult to injury

Time's sea level is rising
I'm preparing to drown

I'm preparing to love water
and to hold my breath

Life etches itself
where love collects

Losing Ground

What used to stop me in my tracks
and threaten to sink me with its impact
now slips away discreetly at night
like Arctic icebergs breaking off
in someone else's proverbial backyard

While true-north poets forget their lines
and oar-less boats turn with the tides
parts of me drift away
in a foreboding and foretold
chain of events

With so much spilled water
I don't want to add tears
or leave innocent children
at the deep end of the world
not able to touch bottom

I Don't Have

I don't have the balm of little children
I don't have an island to go to
I can't build a house or lift heavy loads
I won't drive on I-95

I don't have a garden that doesn't die
that isn't choked out by weeds
at the end of every season

I don't have a brown paper bag or a locker
I don't have a mother or father

I don't have a pen
that writes in many colors
I can't change a tire or hunt

I count on my fingers
and watch the nightly news
I watch falling stars
but don't wish for what isn't

I don't have a lock that is foolproof
I don't have a good sense of direction

I don't want a lawn to take care of
I don't have a neat tied up ending

I don't want advice
to live someone else's life
I don't want the latest panacea

I don't like the sound
of water flooding
or a faucet dripping
like thoughtless talk

Do you mind if I don't tell you
what you don't want to hear?
You spend time
then have none

I don't have a platitude
or a rehearsed answer
I don't want a finish line
or to start over
I don't want the lights
left on all night

Dreams Have No Platitudes

Not dreams as lofty goals
but the unruly kind
that we have at night
when no one is looking

The ones with potency
that are brutally honest
that bypass the vanity
of ego and dogma

Dreams that disturb
and urge self-reflection
are magically empowering
but not politically correct

Buried like bodies
waiting to be claimed
they're odd for a reason
to get our attention

With a maze of meaning
and a poetic license
they cross barriers
and yield to surreal

Immortal, yet fragile
in a shorthand of symbols
they make or break
with no regret
the soul's destiny
the hero's gold

When Sleep Plays Hard to Get

From a promising first impression
to a string of false starts
it's always a blind date
when sleep plays hard to get

When my mind is a bell
I hold back the clapper
and match my breath
with the chant of mantra

While my thoughts wear a path
and count down to the future
They linger and loom
and lead to nowhere

Sometimes I play dead
or toss and turn the other cheek
where the grass is greener
and the sheep have been counted

When sleep is a flirt
that won't commit
and my body is a burden
deprived of slumber

I drown myself
in the need to go under
as I wait for sleep's
sweet amnesia

Stormed -January 2021

The night the world fell apart
it thawed and violently dropped
It snapped and crashed in chunks
and loudly broke its wholeness

Truth clung like polar bears
trying to survive
on floating sidewalks
with tell-tale cracks
While the drone of lies
hummed like a generator
that we hoped
would run out of gas

The truth slept
but had a dream
a casualty count
of a world changed
of gathering storms
that no lives can hide from

of gifts not given
and plans undone
Uprooted and unplugged
from the grace of holy ground
The weight of the world
bore down

This is Not a Horror Movie

Waiting to be snatched
to be left in the woods
with no path back

Waiting to forget
names and faces
to lose your place
and everything you trusted

How will it end?
Asleep in your bed?
Will it come all at once
when you least expect it?

Will we all be picked off
one by one?
Will there be a light?
Will there be blood?

Will we have a caring
hand to hold?
Will we fade
like words on paper
or fall like dominos?

How long before
we'll be forgotten?
Will we go willingly
or will we be taken?

Will our souls exist
once our body has vanished?
Will there be reunions
regrets, relief?

The Magic Trick

It takes years of prep
for the magic trick
of being here one minute
and gone the next

Death is as strange
as being sawed in half
One day your parachute won't open

And on the way down you'll ask
Who was it for?
What was it worth?
Was it believable?

What Would Carl Jung Say?

I dreamt I cut off my ear
the way I casually cut fabric
or slice a potato
which made me ask
What other ways do I self-harm?
What other impulsive act
can't be taken back?
What don't I want to hear?

I saved the evidence
but forgot what it was intended for
so I tucked it into the trash
like a bloody sanitary pad
and hid the shame behind my hair

A gateway to harder partings?
A forgotten trade?
A card laid on the table?
Does it take a death
to generate interest?

'The sadness will last forever'
said Vincent Van Gogh
before he died of a wound made visible
a gamble of high stakes

Do we lose to win
until we have nothing left to give?
Do we pay down our debt
with the parts of our self?

Do we give up our borrowed miracles
while starry night lights go out
while worn-out sunflowers sheepishly bow
and our busywork
winds down?

SUNFLOWERS

I can't stand to see them droop
Faces hung like lamps bent over
Their lights are out

Their shame is as drastic
as their joy was in August
They burn at both ends

Like high summer models in Van Gogh poses
Did their beauty go to their heads?
Or do they bow in humble gestures?

But I can only see what their faces mirror
Fears in me, bent over crones with osteoporosis
pecked out eyes, lost teeth

Did they stand too tall
too long without cover?

I don't grow sunflowers
They're too dramatic
They're easy targets
of nature's wrath

They hang like skulls
in suicide nooses
in garden graveyards
for Halloween

Or stand like crosses
of martyred saviors
with their seed spilled out
like blood

Their thorny crowns
have fallen down
Their bones loom long

As the days close in
like lowered coffins
light abandons me

Winter comes
as a Rumplestilskin
to steal my first born golden son

Faded hope is money spent
Now we are poor with no mothers
Now we are old with only mortal gods
and rent to pay for all we have loved

Ashes to ashes
We knew this would happen
But we never want it to be now

I keep the memory of sunflowers
on refrigerator magnets
next to bright shiny photographs
from when my children were young

When You Come Full Circle

When references expire and culture sours
you don't teach an old dog new tricks
You keep a lifeline up your sleeve
Pray not to trip and fall over

When strippers win Grammys
And rappers praise their crotches
You wonder what it will be like
to be put out to pasture

You look like your mother
and are proud of it
You play hooky from timeclocks
and still read the beatniks

You can still speak gibberish
But not emoji
You LOL
and mute the rest

You make your own bed
but don't do the dishes
Your knees buckle
and your implants are teeth

When bells and whistles
replace on and off switches
you wait for bluebirds
and make final playlist wishes

You forget pans
burning on the stove
but not the nursery rhymes
that you learned long ago

You come full circle
You're all thumbs
You blush and stutter
and hold it in

When temperatures rise
and standards fall
You don't make promises
or wait for saviors

Your rules are still golden
but sticks and stones can leave you broken
You take advice from children
You're more like them now

Hit Publish

Don't be a falling star
without a wish
Don't pull the rug out
from under someone
and call it musical chairs

Hide a rhyme
Break into a poem
Spend time in the dark room
to develop your life

Save the Sunday ashes
of your burned down house
Dig deeper
Plant an idea

Don't paint soup cans
Don't rehearse
Don't buy Boardwalk
It's over rated

And Baltic Ave
is too cheap

Just When I Think I Have No More Poems to Write

When poetry becomes dictation
it's like having an imaginary friend
that no one (but you) believes in
and no one wants to meet

When poetry becomes a distraction
it's like holding your ear towards the moon
and listening for the ocean
where everyone knows
the sky should be

Open Slowly

Poetry is a reverse psychology
A Van Gogh gold mother lode
turned starry night

Read from a mirror
in a rear view
Tied together
with a strand of moon

It's a lost and found letter
returned to its sender
Dream delivered
Truth unsealed

Look Away

A poem is like the sun
that you can only take in doses
that you can't look at directly
or force to shine
It's a gold star charm
A bright idea to follow
flashing insights
and casting shadows
as its good luck
comes and goes

When We Wait More Than We Write

When our eyes become
adjusted to darkness
we call ourselves poets

The ones who stand
too close to the speakers
listening for the hum
of the world's forgotten song

We wait for falling stars
to burn in our laps
for dread to pass
and time to stop

We wear berets
and quit our jobs
fix our gaze
on the faraway

We empty our pockets
and give up our turn
We sit in moonlight
and tie up loose ends

We wait for poems
that fit like skin
We dream them
from a distance
then write them
close in

Decomposition

I hate when a notebook ends
It's like a detour in the road
when I don't know the alternate route

If a notebook was a casket
I would recite the best parts
and read a funeral eulogy
before I closed the cover

I would bury it in my yard
like a dog buries a bone
then forgets to dig it up
and moves on

It fills up too fast
like your child grows up
like your teenaged grandchild
resists your affection

An old journal's like a closet
for all your favorite outfits
mixed in with all the misfits
that only take up space

A new journal is stiff
like tight clothes that don't fit
because one size never fits all
and they only make has-been
high-rise jeans now

The Older Poet

I can't drink tea
on an empty stomach
Can't bring lilacs in the house
because the fragrance is too strong

When my husband gets bored and restless
he thinks about changing jobs
I just change the color of my nightgown
But is has to be silk

Let It Be

Now I have to learn to nap
and wake up three times a night
Now I have to talk to bag boys
at the grocery store
who don't know who wrote Let It Be

I talk to the flowers in my garden
I call them 'my beautiful girls'
I hang out with friends that play Scrabble
and hang up on the automated voices
that tell me how the menu has changed

Now I lose names and forget passwords
but not the lyrics to every song I've loved
Now past and present, losses and blessings
exist together, all at once

When Time Doesn't Rhyme

You like to rhyme time
and make it seem natural
You make the best of chaos
and confront your denial

You leave your will and testament
with every written poem
You read newspaper obituaries
as if looking for your next home room

You hurt your knees
scrubbing kitchen floors
You gave up praying on them
years ago

You wear your beret
in your imaginary coffin
while your husband rests in trees
where wildlife consumes him

You regret not sending
a message in a bottle
dug from a backyard dump
from before there was plastic

Birds are your angels now
You practice to be one
You save your voice
and hold out for an heirloom

You vow not to forget
love's lasting imprint
when life has been spent
and time no longer counts you

You Are Here

Our bodies are like maps
on dog-eared pages
marked by old haunts
across sun freckled flesh

Stretched with furrowed plots
down travel-logged paths
where bones bend like branches
under the weight of fruitful days

Our bodies wane translucent
Our veins bulge blue
Sharp edges soften
and thoughts slow with overuse

Until our view turns inward
to off-the-map futures
where our bodies are the breath
that carries on and echoes

Where our bodies are the stories
that linger when they're spoken
that live beyond bound matter
and the fear of being forgotten

The Scenic Route
For my children

Sorrow is a beautiful country
where you meet your destiny

where your foundation of love
holds immense treasure
when you trust the lay of its land

Because its depth is as far as its width
and its jewel is disguised by darkness

You have to dig deep to mine its value
to bear and wear its shine

ASHES TO ASHES

If something burns your soul with purpose and desire, it's your duty to be reduced to ashes by it. - Charles Bukowski

I saw my life in a box
of mementos and photos
and outdated clothes
that nobody wants

A cardboard collection
extensions of self
of props and scraps
that defend my existence
and memories like atoms
that hold me together

They fade but I cling
I hoard and remember
They pile up like the newspapers
At my dead brother's door

Yellowing proof
Destined for worm food
My life flashed before me
is yesterday's news

I imagine skimming parts
that rise to the surface
and organizing my life
like a table of contents

I'm a name, date and number
with a legacy of chapters
in a story that will never
be told the same twice

Delete and donate
Don't burden the planet
Angels are in the attic
sorting someone's thrift shop finds

The birds are my angels
Their old songs are new
I tell time through the windows
by the flowers that are in bloom

I saw my life in a box
like a cold case
crushed like diamonds
in a buried fortune
distilled like a body
in a funeral vase

How to Die

Start early
Don't leave it
to the last minute
Pull up a chair
and watch what happens
Don't forget to breathe
before you stop breathing
Don't leave without saying goodbye

Hibernation 2020

I'm hibernating
but keeping good company
with invisible essentials
from waking dreams

With the snap of fingers
comes a ghost dance inventory
while one day bleeds
and the next is saved

From a paint box sun
with paper and pen
words on pages
take names

With no expectations
and a to-do list erased
I'm getting used to
not being seen

The Last Dance

When the soul asserts
its right of way
it leads the dance

Grief and honoring
are the blood sisters
that braid the steps

They slow-dance through loss
hold the symmetry of paradox
and for the sake of artful fate
are moved towards transcendence

When the soul takes the lead
there's a deep delving
There's a widening horizon
with the narrowing of life

There's a fading of resistance
with the diminishing of endurance
There's a honing of timing
a falling into place

The Final Leaving: How to

Pack it up
Sell off the parts
Let it drop

Become a disembodied name
that slips the mind
Fall out of character

Start at the end
and take a number
Walk through walls
or walk on water

Become the air
for others to breathe
A memory that floats
like a fragrance

Surprise Endings

It takes effort
to adjust my pace
to follow the beat
and not lose my place

I'm not a leader
or a follower
I'm a single wallflower
that learned to bloom
that moves to the rhythm
of the seasons
and retreats in solitude

I close my eyes to see
until the drum is silenced
until life's puzzle is nearly finished
and I can add my piece to the whole

But don't look too close
or you'll miss the full picture
where everyone is a beautiful loner
where we all belong to each other
are the parts of the same single truth

About the Author

Colleen Redman grew up as one of nine siblings on a peninsula in the South Shore of Boston, MA during the '50s - '60s. Since 1991, she has lived with her husband in a cabin off the scenic Blue Ridge Parkway in Floyd, a rural Virginia county known for its mountain culture, roots music, small farm homesteads and a flourishing art scene. She has two grown sons and two grandsons, keeps a small flock of chickens and tends a large garden. She is a blogger (looseleafnotes.com) who has written and photographed extensively for The *Floyd Press* newspaper and other regional publications. Her poetry has most recently been published in the *Artemis Journal* and *Floyd County Moonshine*.

Losing two brothers a month apart in 2001 was a life-changing event that spurred Redman's study of death and was the impetus behind her 2003 book The Jim and Dan Stories, which was included in a curriculum for a Radford University grief and loss class for counselors before it went out of print. With the loss of her brothers, Redman let herself descend into "the trenches of grief's front line." She wrote, "If I can describe what I see from inside this hole, will it help others when they are down in one? What place is this? How deep does it go? I want to know. I've never been here before." Her brothers' deaths were followed by the passing of her father, her older sister and mother.

In 2017, Redman's poetry collection *Packing a Suitcase for the Afterlife* was published by Finishing Line Press and reviewed by poet and creative writing teacher Felicia Mitchell: "She has, paradoxically, told the untold, touching on that which resides both in dreams and in life and in the borders between..." Poet and novelist Jim Minick wrote: "Loss tempered by wonder, love radiating like the moon (a bowl fired by the sun"), these poems track a life, playful yet dark, frank and funny, yet somber..."

Packing a Suitcase for the Afterlife was followed by the 2021 publication of *Objects are Closer Than They Appear*, described by the poet as "a distillation through the rear-view mirror of poetic memoir where every remnant pulled from a dream or a memory resonates with an afterlife, as if a visitation from the same place my dead loved ones are, closer than they seem."

As with her first two poetry collections, the poems that appear in *Poems from the Dark Room* are the basis of Redman's "Grief and Relief: Soulful Aging Tour," the call-and-response poetry readings that she does with fellow poet and author of *Poetic Memoir of a Nascent Senescent*, Katherine Chantal. They represent a deepening and a charting of the inner-life adventure, one that has come closest to touching and trusting the mysteries of life and death, one that brings the grace of grief full circle.

You vow not to forget
love's lasting imprint
when life has been spent
and time no longer counts you...

ACKNOWLEDGMENTS

Poems from the Dark Room first appeared in the 2022 issue of *Artemis Journal*
Hibernation was published in *Floyd County Moonshine*, Winter 2021

Made in United States
Troutdale, OR
12/14/2023